LORD, SHOW US THY FACE
AND
WE SHALL BE SAVED

A Mission of Light,

Truth and Transformation

Allan Smith

Published by: Bishop Sheen Today
www.bishopsheentoday.com

Scripture quotations in this book are taken from the Revised Standard Version – Catholic Edition, Second Edition (RSV-2CE).

Archbishop Fulton J. Sheen himself often quoted from the Douay-Rheims Bible; this edition uses the RSV-2CE for clarity while preserving the devotional tone of his insights.

Title: Lord, show us Thy Face and We Shall Be Saved. A Mission of light, truth, and transformation.

Compiled by Allan J. Smith. Includes bibliographical references.

Book formatting and design by Ajayi Isaac
mailto:smeplegacy@gmail.com/ +2348162435897

Identifiers:

Paperback: 978-1-997627-99-9
eBook: 978-1-997627-70-8
Hardcover: 978-1-997931-05-8

Subjects: Jesus Christ — The Holy Hour — Prayer and Meditation — Eucharistic Adoration — Sacred Scripture — The Holy Face Devotion — St. Thérèse of Lisieux — Archbishop Fulton J. Sheen — Lives of the Saints

LORD, SHOW US THY FACE
AND WE SHALL BE SAVED
A Mission of Light, Truth, and Transformation
A Sheen Mission Series - Volume IV

The Sheen Mission Series invites you to walk with Archbishop Fulton J. Sheen in prayer, reparation, and renewal — a journey of the Holy Face, the Cross, the Eucharist, and Our Blessed Mother.

Description:

Lord, Show Us Thy Face and We Shall Be Saved is the fourth volume in the Sheen Mission Series — a mission of light, truth, and transformation centred on the Eucharist and the Face of Christ.

This book gathers Sheen's reflections on Eucharistic adoration, the call to reparation, and the power of Christ's Face to renew hearts and heal the world. It is both a prayer manual and a missionary summons — inviting every soul to be transformed by the radiance of Christ's presence.

Series Note:

This book is the final volume in *The Sheen Mission Series,* a collection of spiritual companions for personal devotion and parish renewal:

"The Face of Christ is the Gospel made visible.
To contemplate His Face is to contemplate the love that saves the world."

— Archbishop Fulton J. Sheen

Dedication:

**To Our Lady of the Holy Name of God
who first gazed upon The Face of Christ**

&

**To Archbishop Fulton J. Sheen,
whose voice still calls us to adore Him.**

J M J

Archbishop Fulton J. Sheen often reminded us that the world will not be saved by diplomacy or politics, but by a return to Christ in the Eucharist. His life and mission proclaimed the central truth: *"The greatest love story of all time is contained in a tiny white Host."*

This fourth volume in the *Sheen Mission Series* continues his call to Eucharistic reparation and adoration. It gathers reflections that invite us to gaze upon the Face of Christ, discover His presence in the Blessed Sacrament, and embrace His call to holiness through prayer, sacrifice, and evangelization.

The aims of this devotional mission are threefold: to foster a deeper love for the Eucharist, to encourage regular adoration before the Blessed Sacrament, and to inspire the faithful to bring Christ's light and truth into the world. Alongside Sheen's wisdom, readers will find traditional prayers and devotions to strengthen their Eucharistic life.

It is my prayer that these pages will lead you into the silence of adoration, where the Face of Christ is revealed in mystery and mercy. There, at His altar-throne, may you encounter His transforming love and carry it into your daily life.

Archbishop Sheen once said that "books are the most patient of teachers." May this one be a patient companion for you, guiding your heart ever closer to Christ, present in the Eucharist, the Light of the World.

Sit Nomen Domini Benedictum!

Blessed be the Name of the Lord!

Allan J. Smith

October 3, 2025

Feast of St. Thérèse of the Child Jesus and the Holy Face. Patron Saint of the foreign missions and priests.

Table of Contents

xvi

Preface

There is a prayer that rises like incense from the pages of the Psalms: *"Restore us, O Lord; let Your Face shine, that we may be saved."* (Psalm 80:3) It is a prayer that expresses the deepest longing of the human heart — the desire to see God, to be seen by Him, and to live in the light of His countenance.

This volume, the fourth and final in the *Sheen Mission Series*, is built upon that cry. It is a meditation on the Face of Christ — the Face that reveals the invisible God, the Face that shone in Bethlehem, wept in Gethsemane, bled on Calvary, and now radiates in glory from the Eucharist. To seek His Face is to seek salvation. To contemplate His countenance is to find peace.

Archbishop Fulton J. Sheen, whose life and teaching inspire this series, never tired of proclaiming that Christianity is not an idea but a Person — the living Christ who meets us face to Face. In every Holy Hour, Sheen adored that Face hidden in the Eucharist, and from that contemplation drew the strength to preach Christ to millions. He understood that evangelization begins in adoration, and that the transformation of the world begins with the transformation of the soul before God.

This book follows that path. It begins with the revelation of Christ's Face in the Incarnation, shines with the radiance of the Eucharist, and leads us through the mystery of reparation, the darkness of the Cross, the light of the Church, and the quiet transformation of contemplation. Each chapter is a step along the way of seeking His countenance more deeply, so that we may also reflect it more faithfully to others.

The *Sheen Mission Series* began with the **Holy Face and the Little Way**, guiding us with St. Thérèse of Lisieux to console and love Christ in reparation. It led us to **Behold Your Mother**, where Mary's sorrowful and tender gaze taught us to stand at the foot of the Cross. It brought us to **The Cross and the Last Words**, where Sheen himself became our companion at Calvary, opening the treasures of Christ's dying words. And now, in this final volume, it gathers all together in a single plea: *"Lord, show us Thy Face, and we shall be saved."*

This is not merely a conclusion but a sending forth. To contemplate the Face of Christ is to be changed by it. And to be changed by it is to become His Face in the world — radiant with His love, merciful in His name, and steadfast in His truth.

May this book, like the series it completes, draw you into a deeper intimacy with Our Lord. May it inspire you to spend time before His Eucharistic countenance. May it strengthen you in reparation, in mission, in suffering, and in joy. And above all, may it awaken in your heart the great longing that will only be satisfied when at last we see Him face to Face in glory.

Foreword

At the heart of the Church is a mystery both hidden and revealed: the Eucharist. Behind the silence of the tabernacle, behind the veils of bread and wine, dwells the living Christ — His Face radiant with mercy, His Heart burning with love.

Archbishop Fulton J. Sheen often declared that "The greatest love story of all time is contained in a tiny white Host." For over sixty years, he lived this love story daily by keeping a Holy Hour before the Blessed Sacrament. He urged priests, religious, and laypeople alike to do the same, convinced that the renewal of the Church and the healing of the world would come through Eucharistic adoration.

This book — the fourth in the Sheen Mission Series — continues that call. It is an invitation to discover anew the transforming power of the Eucharist, to see the Face of Christ in the Host, and to allow His Presence to change your life.

Sheen reminded us that before we can bring Christ to others, we must first spend time with Him ourselves. Adoration is not wasted time; it is the source of all fruitfulness. From silence before the Eucharist flows strength for mission, clarity for discernment, and courage for sacrifice.

May these pages draw you into that silence, where the Face of Christ shines most brightly. And may they help you discover what Sheen himself discovered: that in adoration, we do not merely look at Christ — we are looked upon by Him.

Introduction:
Why the Eucharist? Why Now?

Why the Eucharist? Because it is Christ Himself, given to us as food for the journey. Because in the Host, we encounter the same Jesus who walked the roads of Galilee, who died upon the Cross, and who now reigns in glory. The Eucharist is not a symbol, but the living Presence of the Lord, Emmanuel — God with us.

Why now? Because our world is starving. In an age of noise, distraction, and unbelief, countless souls long for meaning and intimacy but seek it in places that cannot satisfy. Archbishop Sheen saw clearly that "the world is not dying for want of knowledge; it is dying for want of love." That love is found, above all, in the Eucharist.

This fourth volume in the Sheen Mission Series brings together reflections and prayers that lead us to the altar, the monstrance, and the tabernacle. Its aim is threefold:

- To foster a deeper love for the Eucharist as the center of Christian life.

3

- To encourage regular adoration before the Blessed Sacrament.
- To inspire a spirit of mission, bringing Christ's light and truth into the world.

It is my prayer that this book will help you fall in love with Christ anew in the Eucharist. May you discover, in the silence of adoration, that the Face of Christ shines not only upon the altar, but also upon your heart.

For the words of the Psalmist remain true: "Let Your Face shine, that we may be saved." (Psalm 80:3)

The Light of His Face

There is a cry that runs through all of Scripture: *"Let Your face shine upon us, Lord, and we shall be saved."* (Psalm 80:3) From the Old Testament psalmist to the disciples who longed to see Christ, the human heart has always yearned for the Face of God. In Jesus Christ, that longing is fulfilled. His is the Face that reveals the invisible God, the countenance that radiates mercy, the visage that endured spittle and thorns, and the glory that shines brighter than the sun at His Resurrection.

Archbishop Fulton J. Sheen often reminded us that Christianity is not a philosophy, but a Person — a living Christ who gazes upon us in love. To contemplate His Face is to enter into that love. To adore Him in the

Eucharist is to be bathed in the radiance of His presence. To make reparation is to console the Face that was disfigured for our sake.

This volume, the final in the *Sheen Mission Series*, is both a prayer and a summons. It is an invitation to let the Eucharist become the light of your soul, to see in Mary the reflection of her Son's Face, and to bring that radiance into the darkness of the world. It is a call to reparation, but also to transformation. For when the world looks upon our lives, it must not see us alone — it must see the Face of Christ shining through us.

Let us then take up the ancient cry: *"Lord, show us Thy Face, and we shall be saved."*

Chapter One:
The Face of Christ Revealed

Before the coming of Christ, the world could only glimpse the Face of God in shadows and signs. Moses, who spoke with God as a friend, was told: *"You cannot see My Face, for man shall not see Me and live."* (Exodus 33:20) And yet, from that moment, the prophets continued to speak of a day when the light of God's countenance would be revealed to His people.

In the Incarnation, this promise is fulfilled. The eternal Word takes flesh, and for the first time in history, the Face of God is visible. The Child of Bethlehem, wrapped in swaddling clothes, bears the same countenance that will later shine on Mount Tabor and bleed on Calvary. To gaze upon the Infant is already to gaze upon the Redeemer.

Archbishop Fulton J. Sheen often said that God became visible so that we might fall in love with Him. The eyes of Christ look upon us not with judgment but with mercy. His smile is the smile of the Father's love. His tears are the tears of divine compassion. Every feature of His Face reveals the mystery of a God who chose to be known, not as an abstract idea, but as a living Friend.

The world today is hungry for this revelation. Faces surround us on every screen, yet they rarely reflect the peace and love for which the soul longs. Only one Face can satisfy the human heart. Only one countenance can restore the world's lost hope. That is the Face of Christ, radiant in the Eucharist, shining in the saints, and calling to each of us: *"Seek My Face."*

To begin this mission, then, is to make a resolution of the heart: that above all other desires, we will seek the Face of Christ. For in seeking Him, we shall find salvation.

Chapter Two:
The Eucharist: Radiance of His Presence

When Philip said to Jesus, *"Lord, show us the Father, and we shall be satisfied"* (John 14:8), he voiced the cry of every human heart. Our Lord's reply was simple and stunning: *"He who has seen Me has seen the Father."* To see the Face of Christ is to behold the Father's love. And nowhere is that love more radiant, more tangible, than in the Eucharist.

The Eucharist is not merely a symbol or reminder. It is Christ Himself — Body, Blood, Soul, and Divinity — veiled under the appearance of bread and wine. Yet though veiled, He is not hidden. His Real Presence shines through to the eyes of faith. The Host may seem humble, but for those who adore Him, it is nothing less than the Face of Christ turned toward His people.

Archbishop Fulton J. Sheen once said that every Holy Hour is an hour spent "looking at Him and letting Him look at you." This is the essence of Eucharistic adoration: a meeting of gazes. We look upon the Host, and though we see only whiteness, our faith tells us that the Face of Christ is there — the same Face that once smiled upon the leper, wept over Jerusalem, and shone with glory at the Resurrection. In return, He looks upon us with eyes that know our hearts, that pierce through our sins, that radiate mercy.

To kneel before the tabernacle or monstrance is therefore to step into the light of His countenance. It is to allow His radiance to penetrate the shadows within us. Like the sun shining on a darkened room, His Eucharistic Presence illumines our souls, revealing both the dust of sin and the beauty of grace. We cannot remain unchanged when exposed to such light.

The world desperately needs this radiance. Surrounded by the artificial glow of screens, many souls grow dim with fatigue and despair. But Christ's Eucharistic light is not artificial; it is eternal. It restores, renews, and enkindles. To bring the world back to life, Catholics must once again be reflectors of that light, carrying it from the altar into every corner of society.

The Eucharist is therefore not only the radiance of Christ's presence — it is also the radiance of our mission. To adore Him is to be transformed by Him. To receive Him is to become like Him. To look upon His Face in the Host is to learn how to be His Face for others.

Let us then resolve to return often to the Eucharist. Let us spend time in the light of His Presence, until our lives, too, begin to glow with His love. For only those who have reflected His radiance can become, in Sheen's words, "Christ-bearers to the world."

Chapter Three:
Reparation: Love's Response

Love, when it sees that it has wounded the Beloved, seeks to make amends. This is the essence of reparation. It is not a cold duty or grim obligation, but the spontaneous movement of a heart pierced by love. When we realize that our sins have struck the Face of Christ, bruised and spat upon, we cannot remain indifferent. Love compels us to console Him.

Archbishop Fulton J. Sheen often reminded us that sin is not merely the breaking of a law, but the wounding of a Person. Every sin is a turning away from the Face of Christ. Yet every act of reparation is a turning back, a way of saying, *"Lord, I am sorry. I love You. Let me share in Your sorrow so that I may share in Your joy."*

The saints understood this. St. Thérèse of Lisieux, who united her Little Way to the devotion of the Holy Face, longed to wipe away the tears of Jesus with her small sacrifices. St. Veronica, on the road to Calvary, braved the jeers of the crowd to press her veil to His blood-stained Face. Each act of reparation, great or small, becomes a caress upon the wounds of Christ.

Reparation is not confined to heroic deeds; it can be woven into the fabric of daily life. A hidden prayer offered for those who blaspheme, an act of patience in the face of provocation, an hour of adoration before the Eucharist — all these are ways of repairing for the coldness and ingratitude that Our Lord suffers. Every act of love is like a drop of balm upon His wounds.

Why is reparation needed? Because love demands it, and because souls depend on it. Sheen often compared reparation to standing in the breach: when sin threatens to overwhelm the world, the reparative soul intercedes, offering love where hatred abounds, light where darkness spreads. Reparation is participation in the very mission of Christ, who offered Himself as the ultimate act of love to heal the broken bond between God and man.

The Face of Christ, once disfigured by sin, now shines with the glory of forgiveness. To console Him in His suffering is to share in His triumph. And as we make reparation, we ourselves are transformed. Our hearts grow tender, our love more selfless, our gaze more fixed on His.

Let us then embrace reparation, not with fear, but with joy. For in repairing the wounds of Christ, we learn the deepest secret of love: that when we give Him our little acts of sorrow, He returns to us the radiance of His smile.

Chapter Four:
The Light that Shines in Darkness

From the opening of St. John's Gospel, we hear the promise: *"The light shines in the darkness, and the darkness has not overcome it."* (John 1:5) Christ is that light. His Face is the radiance of God shining into the shadows of a fallen world. And yet, the mystery of our faith is that this light is revealed most powerfully in moments of suffering, trial, and apparent defeat.

Look to Calvary. The sky darkens, the earth trembles, and all seems lost. Yet in the midst of this darkness, the crucified Face of Christ shines with the brightest love. His eyes, though dimmed with blood, radiate forgiveness. His lips, parched with thirst, proclaim mercy. His countenance, marred beyond recognition, is at the same time the most radiant revelation of God's glory.

Archbishop Fulton J. Sheen often said that the Cross is like a blackboard upon which God wrote His deepest lesson: that love is stronger than hate, that life conquers death, that light is never extinguished by darkness. The Cross does not hide the Face of Christ; it reveals it.

Our world today knows much darkness. The shadow of unbelief, the weight of sin, the wounds of division and violence — all threaten to obscure hope. And yet, precisely in these moments, the light of Christ shines most clearly. Every soul that turns in faith to His Eucharistic Presence, every act of reparation, every prayer whispered in love — these are sparks of light piercing the night.

It is not only the great saints who bear this light. Every Christian, by baptism, is called to reflect the Face of Christ in a world desperate for hope. In the patient endurance of suffering, in the courage to forgive, in the quiet witness of prayer, the light of His countenance shines through us. As Sheen said, "The greatest contribution we can make to the world is to let Christ shine through us."

To live in the light of Christ's Face is therefore not to escape the world's darkness but to transform it. We carry His radiance not by fleeing from the Cross but by embracing it. In doing so, our own faces become illumined, so that even in trial, others may see in us a reflection of the One who said: *I am the Light of the world. Whoever follows Me will not walk in darkness, but will have the light of life.*" (John 8:12)

Let us then walk with confidence into the world's shadows, not with fear, but with the certainty that the light of Christ's Face shines through us. For the darker the night, the more brightly His countenance is revealed.

Chapter Five:
The Mission of Evangelization

When Philip once cried, *"Lord, show us the Father, and we shall be satisfied"* (John 14:8), he expressed not only a personal longing but the desire of every soul. The Face of Christ is the answer to that desire. To contemplate Him in adoration is to be filled; to proclaim Him in mission is to share that fullness with the world. Evangelization, then, is nothing less than reflecting His Face so that others may see and believe.

Archbishop Fulton J. Sheen was above all a missionary. Whether speaking to millions on the radio, preaching in cathedrals, or visiting the poor, his one goal was to make the Face of Christ visible to the world. He often reminded us that people today listen not so much to arguments as to witnesses. The truest evangelist is the one whose life shines with the radiance of Christ's countenance.

This mission begins in silence before the Eucharist. To bring Christ to the world, we must first be transformed by gazing upon Him ourselves. Sheen would spend his Holy Hour each day not as preparation for preaching, but as communion with the Lord. Yet it was in that silence that the fire of his words was kindled. Evangelization flows from adoration. We cannot show the Face of Christ unless we have first sought it.

The world longs for this witness. In an age of masks, when faces are often hidden behind distractions, divisions, and despair, the Church is called to reveal the true Face of hope. Evangelization is not merely programs or strategies; it is the shining forth of Christ's love through lives that have been illumined by Him. Every Christian is a missionary. Every parish is a mission station. Every home can be a beacon of His light.

To evangelize is also to repair the image of God in souls disfigured by sin. Just as Veronica's veil bore the imprint of Christ's suffering Face, so our witness is meant to impress His image upon others. By words of truth, by deeds of mercy, by the patient endurance of trials, we leave behind the living imprint of His love.

The task may seem daunting, but Sheen would remind us that God needs only willing instruments. The world does not expect us to be brilliant; it expects us to be radiant. It does not require us to have all the answers; it longs to see in us the Face of Christ.

Let us then accept the mission of evangelization with courage. Let us gaze upon His Face in the Eucharist until our own faces are transfigured with His light. And then, like Moses descending from the mountain, let us go forth so that all who meet us may see reflected, however dimly, the radiance of the One who saves.

Chapter Six:
Mary, Mirror of the Face of Christ

When a child is born, those who gather around the crib often remark: *"He has his mother's eyes... her smile... her face."* In the mystery of the Incarnation, it was the opposite that was true. The Face of Christ bore the likeness of His Mother. The eternal Word took flesh from Mary, and the human features that revealed the invisible God were fashioned in her womb.

Mary is therefore the first and most perfect mirror of the Face of Christ. To look upon her is to see the reflection of her Son; to draw near to her is to be led unfailingly to Him. As Archbishop Fulton J. Sheen often said, *"Never do we honour Mary more than when we speak of her as pointing the way to her Son."*

At Bethlehem, she gazed with love upon His newborn Face. At Nazareth, she saw the smile of God in the boy who was her Child and her Lord. On Calvary, her eyes met His eyes as His countenance was disfigured by suffering. Through it all, she remained faithful, holding in her heart the vision of His Face even when it was hidden from the world.

Mary also reflects Christ's light to us. Just as the moon has no light of its own but shines with the radiance of the sun, so Mary's beauty comes entirely from her union with her Son. She is the "Woman clothed with the sun" (Revelation 12:1), whose very being magnifies the Lord. When we see her tenderness, we glimpse the mercy of Christ. When we behold her purity, we perceive the holiness of Christ. When we experience her intercession, we feel the compassion of Christ.

This is why devotion to Mary is never a distraction but always a safeguard of true faith. She magnifies Christ. She teaches us how to gaze upon His Face with love, how to endure suffering with Him, how to reflect His light in a dark world. Every genuine Marian devotion is a pathway to deeper contemplation of Christ.

For this reason, reparation to the Holy Face is inseparable from devotion to the Sorrowful Mother. Just as she once wiped the blood from His countenance on the road to Calvary through Veronica's veil, so now she teaches us to console Him with our prayers and sacrifices. She is the first disciple of the Holy Face, and she continues to form us as her children in this school of love.

Let us then turn to Mary with confidence. In her, we will see reflected the very Face we long to behold. And as we walk with her, she will gently teach us to become mirrors ourselves — reflecting Christ to others until the whole world is illumined with His light.

Chapter Seven:
The Cross and the Glory of His Face

The Gospels tell us that as Christ hung upon the Cross, *"there was darkness over the whole land"* (Matthew 27:45). To the world, it appeared that His Face was disfigured, His mission defeated, His light extinguished. Yet for those with eyes of faith, this was not defeat but triumph. The Cross is the throne from which Christ reigns, and His marred countenance is the very revelation of God's glory.

Archbishop Fulton J. Sheen often said that the world's idea of glory is power, prestige, and success. God's idea of glory is sacrifice, humility, and love. On Calvary, Christ's Face — bruised, spit upon, crowned with thorns — revealed a beauty the world had never seen: the beauty of love willing to suffer for the beloved. This is the glory of the Cross.

The prophet Isaiah foresaw it: *"He had no form or comeliness that we should look at Him, and no beauty that we should desire Him"* (Isaiah 53:2). Yet hidden beneath the bruises was the splendour of divine mercy. What appeared to be ugliness was in truth the most radiant beauty, for it was the beauty of a God who loves without measure.

At Calvary, Mary's eyes met the eyes of her Son. In that exchange of sorrow and love, the glory of the Cross was already beginning to shine. Mary did not look away from the disfigured Face of Christ; she adored it. So too must we. The world flees from suffering, but the Christian sees in it the very place where God's glory is revealed.

This mystery transforms our own crosses. When trials mar the "face" of our lives, when suffering leaves us scarred, we are tempted to believe that God has abandoned us. But it is precisely then that His glory can shine through us most powerfully. For every act of patient endurance, every offering of sorrow united to His, becomes a reflection of the beauty of the Crucified Face.

The Cross, then, is not the eclipse of God's glory but its revelation. It teaches us that true beauty is sacrificial love, and true victory is found in surrender. When we look upon a crucifix, we see not merely a man condemned but God enthroned. His crown of thorns is His crown of majesty; His broken Face is the radiant icon of divine mercy.

Let us therefore not turn away from the Cross. Let us gaze upon the glory of His Face, even when it is marred by suffering. For there we will learn the deepest truth: that every wound borne in love becomes radiant, every tear shed in faith becomes luminous, and every cross embraced with Christ becomes a share in His eternal glory.

Chapter Eight:
The Church: His Face in the World

When Christ ascended into heaven, His visible presence was withdrawn. Yet He did not leave the world without His Face. He entrusted His presence to the Church, which is His Body, His Bride, and His visible sign in history. Through the Church, Christ continues to look upon the world with eyes of mercy, to speak with words of truth, and to shine with the radiance of His countenance.

Archbishop Fulton J. Sheen loved to call the Church "Christ prolonging Himself in time and space." To encounter the Church is to encounter Christ — sometimes through her sacraments, sometimes through her teaching, sometimes through the simple witness of ordinary believers. Though imperfect in her human members, the Church remains the sacrament of Christ's Face to the nations.

The Eucharist is the most radiant expression of this mystery. Every Mass is a moment when Christ once again shows His Face to the world, hidden yet real, veiled yet radiant. But the Church also reveals His countenance through her works of mercy. When the hungry are fed, the sick visited, the poor uplifted, the forgotten consoled, the world glimpses the compassion etched upon His Face.

Fulton Sheen often reminded us that the greatest scandal in the Church is not her weakness but her failure to reflect Christ. When Christians become disfigured by pride, division, or sin, the world turns away in disappointment, for it does not see the Face it longs to see. But when Christians live with humility, charity, and joy, even the most skeptical hearts can be won.

This is why every believer shares responsibility for the Church's witness. We are each called to be the "face" of Christ in our homes, our parishes, our workplaces. In our patience, people must see His patience; in our forgiveness, His mercy; in our love, His love. As St. Teresa of Avila once wrote: *"Christ has no body now but yours, no hands, no feet on earth but yours."* In the same way, we might say: Christ has no visible Face now but yours.

To belong to the Church is therefore not merely to carry a name but to carry a mission: to let Christ's countenance shine through us so clearly that others may recognize Him. In an age darkened by confusion and division, the world needs once again to see the luminous unity of Christ's Body, the serene beauty of His Bride, and the radiant witness of His saints.

Let us not be ashamed, then, of our identity as members of His Church. Let us show the world the true Face of Christ — in the sacraments we celebrate, in the love we live, and in the hope we proclaim. For when the Church reflects His countenance, the world sees not merely an institution, but the living Face of the Saviour.

Chapter Nine:
Transformation Through Contemplation

To gaze upon the Face of Christ is not a passive act. It is an encounter that changes us. Just as Moses descended Mount Sinai with his face shining after speaking with God, so too the Christian who spends time before the Eucharist carries away the radiance of that divine encounter.

Archbishop Fulton J. Sheen called this the "Law of Transformation." In his words, *"We become like those with whom we associate, and if we associate with Christ in the Blessed Sacrament, we will become like Him."* This is the secret of contemplation: by fixing our eyes on Him, we slowly begin to reflect what we see.

The world often tells us that to be transformed we must strive harder, achieve more, or reinvent ourselves. But true transformation does not come from self-improvement; it comes from self-surrender. The soul that kneels quietly before the tabernacle, day after day, is silently remade. Pride gives way to humility, fear to trust, selfishness to love. Without fanfare or noise, the countenance of Christ begins to shine through the believer.

This is why Eucharistic adoration is not optional for those who wish to live as Christ's witnesses. Evangelization, reparation, mission — all of these are hollow if they are not rooted in the slow, patient work of contemplation. To be Christ's Face in the world, we must first allow His gaze to penetrate us, heal us, and make us new.

The saints bear witness to this transformation. St. Thérèse, gazing upon the crucifix, discovered her Little Way of trust. St. John Vianney, lost in hours of adoration, radiated holiness to his parish. Fulton Sheen himself, faithful to his daily Holy Hour, was able to carry the light of Christ to millions. Their secret was not genius, strategy, or strength. It was simply this: they allowed themselves to be transformed by contemplating His Face.

And this transformation is not for saints alone. Every soul who prays before the Blessed Sacrament enters into the same school of love. Christ does not ask for eloquence or achievement; He asks only for our presence. As we sit in silence, He works in us. As we remain faithful, He reshapes us. As we look upon Him, He makes His Face shine within us.

This is the destiny of every Christian: not merely to admire Christ from afar, but to become His living image. The world is waiting for such souls — men and women whose faces bear the quiet glow of one who has been with the Lord.

Let us then commit ourselves to contemplation. Let us take time each day to seek His Face, not rushing, not demanding, but resting in His presence. For those who contemplate His countenance will themselves be transformed into His likeness, until at last we shall see Him face to Face in glory.

Chapter Ten:
Lord, Show Us Thy Face
and We Shall Be Saved

The ancient cry of Israel has become the cry of the Church: *"Lord, show us Thy Face, and we shall be saved."* (Psalm 80:3) This longing echoes through every page of Scripture, every devotion of the saints, and every hour spent before the tabernacle. It is the cry of the human heart — to see God, to be seen by Him, and to live in the light of His countenance.

In Jesus Christ, this cry has been answered. The Face of the invisible God has been revealed in the Word made flesh. That Face was radiant in Bethlehem, sorrowful on Calvary, glorious in the Resurrection, and now hidden yet present in the Eucharist. To look upon His countenance is to see mercy incarnate, love victorious, hope fulfilled.

Archbishop Fulton J. Sheen taught that the mission of every Christian is to bear this Face to the world. We are not merely disciples but reflectors. Like the moon reflecting the sun, our task is to shine with a light not our own, so that all who look upon us may glimpse the radiance of Christ. Our families, our parishes, our workplaces, our communities — all are waiting for such light.

This mission is not complicated. It begins in adoration. It deepens through reparation. It grows in the silence of contemplation. And it overflows in evangelization, as we bring Christ's love to a world longing for His presence. To seek His Face is to be sent with His Face — to let others encounter Him in our gaze, our words, our actions, and our love.

The journey has brought us here: to the simple but profound truth that salvation is found in the shining of His countenance. And this is not only a hope for the future but a reality for today. Every time we kneel before the Eucharist, every time we whisper a prayer of reparation, every time we show mercy to another, His Face is revealed anew.

One day, this longing will be satisfied in full. The veil will be lifted, and we shall see Him as He is — no longer hidden, no longer in mystery, but face to Face in eternal glory. Until then, we walk by faith, seeking His presence in the Eucharist, in the poor, in the Church, and in one another.

Let us then take up the mission entrusted to us. Let us echo with confidence the cry of the saints, the cry of the Church, the cry of every longing soul:

"Lord, show us Thy Face, and we shall be saved."

Appendix I:
Scripture on the Face of God

Part One: The Old Testament
– The Longing for His Face

- *"The Lord bless you and keep you; the Lord make His Face shine upon you, and be gracious to you; the Lord lift up His countenance upon you, and give you peace."*
— **Numbers 6:24–26**

- *"You have said, 'Seek My Face.' My heart says to You, 'Your Face, Lord, do I seek.'"*
— **Psalm 27:8**

- *"Restore us, O Lord God of hosts; let Your Face shine, that we may be saved."*
— **Psalm 80:19**

- *"Make Your Face shine upon Your servant, and teach me Your statutes."*
— **Psalm 119:135**

- *"Seek the Lord and His strength; seek His presence continually."*
— **1 Chronicles 16:11**

- *"My soul thirsts for God, for the living God. When shall I come and behold the Face of God?"*
  — **Psalm 42:2**

Part Two: The New Testament
– The Face Revealed in Christ

- *"And the Word became flesh and dwelt among us, and we have seen His glory, glory as of the only Son from the Father, full of grace and truth."*
  — **John 1:14**

- *"He who has seen Me has seen the Father."*
  — **John 14:9**

- *"And He was transfigured before them, and His Face shone like the sun, and His clothes became white as light."*
  — **Matthew 17:2**

- *"Then they spat in His Face and struck Him; and some slapped Him, saying, 'Prophesy to us, Christ! Who is it that struck You?'"*
  — **Matthew 26:67–68**

- *"But we all, with unveiled face, beholding the glory of the Lord, are being transformed into the same image from one degree of glory to another."*
  — **2 Corinthians 3:18**
- *"For God, who said, 'Let light shine out of darkness,' has shone in our hearts to give the light of the knowledge of the glory of God in the Face of Jesus Christ."*
  — **2 Corinthians 4:6**

- *"They shall see His Face, and His name shall be on their foreheads. And night shall be no more, for the Lord God will be their light."*
  — **Revelation 22:4–5**

Part Three: A Litany of Scripture Verses on the Holy Face

(To be prayed slowly, with response: **"Lord, let the light of Your Face shine upon us."***)*

- "Seek My Face." — *Your Face, Lord, do I seek.* (Psalm 27:8)

- "Make Your Face shine upon Your servant." (Psalm 119:135)

- "Restore us, O Lord; let Your Face shine, that we may be saved." (Psalm 80:3)

- "He who has seen Me has seen the Father." (John 14:9)

- "His Face shone like the sun." (Matthew 17:2)

- "The glory of God shines in the Face of Jesus Christ." (2 Corinthians 4:6)

- "They shall see His Face, and His name shall be on their foreheads." (Revelation 22:4)

Closing Prayer:

Lord Jesus, Your countenance is light and mercy for every soul. Shine upon us in our weakness, forgive our sins, and transform us with Your presence. May our lives reflect Your Face, until at last we see You face to Face in eternal glory. Amen.

Appendix II:
Fulton Sheen on the
Eucharist and Adoration

Part One:

Sheen's Core Themes on the Eucharist

Archbishop Fulton J. Sheen's life was marked by one unbroken devotion: his daily Holy Hour before the Blessed Sacrament. For over sixty years, he kept this appointment with Christ, no matter how busy his schedule or demanding his ministry. In that silent hour, Sheen found the secret of his strength, the fire of his preaching, and the light of his wisdom.

Fulton Sheen insisted that the Eucharist is not a thing but a Person — the living Christ, present in Body, Blood, Soul, and Divinity. To kneel before the tabernacle is to look into the eyes of Jesus, hidden yet radiant. He often said that the greatest tragedy of the modern Church was not persecution but neglect of this Presence. The cure for a weary world, he believed, was a return to the altar — a return to gazing upon the Face of Christ in the Host.

For Fulton Sheen, the Holy Hour was not simply about speaking but about being seen. He encouraged souls to spend time before the Eucharist as lovers spend time together: in silence, in presence, in communion of hearts. "We become like those we love," he taught. "If we love the Eucharist, we will become like Him whom we adore."

Part Two:
A Treasury of Sheen's Words

- *"The greatest love story of all time is contained in a tiny white Host."*
- *"The Holy Hour is a privileged time to grow more into His likeness. We become like those with whom we associate. If we spend time with Christ, we will become like Christ."*
- *"The only reason for doing a Holy Hour is to grow more and more into His likeness. We come not so much to talk as to be looked at by Him."*
- *"As the sun is never diminished by shining on one flower or a million, so Christ's Presence in the Eucharist is never divided. He is fully present to you as if you were the only one in the world."*
- *"When we make a Holy Hour, we are not alone with Christ. The whole Church is present with us, because the Church lives from the Eucharist."*
- *"If we wish to know the Face of Christ, we will find it in the tabernacle. Hidden there, He waits, radiant with love."*

- *"When we are before the Blessed Sacrament, let us open our hearts. Our Lord speaks to us far more in silence than we can ever speak to Him."*
- *"The purpose of the Holy Hour is not to change God, but to change ourselves. We need the Holy Hour as a compass to keep us on the right path."*
- *"The Holy Hour is like an oxygen tank to revive the breath of the Holy Spirit in the midst of the polluted atmosphere of the world."*
- *"If you do not worship God, you will worship something else. The Eucharist is where true worship is restored."*
- *"In the Holy Hour we are not alone with Jesus; we are with the whole Church, adoring Him on behalf of those who do not."*
- *"The greatest love we can show to others is to bring them into the presence of the Eucharist."*

Part Three:
Praying with Sheen before the Eucharist

Themes for Reflection

1. **Presence** – Christ is not a memory, but truly present in the Eucharist.

   Kneel quietly before the tabernacle or monstrance. Begin with Sheen's prayer:

   "Lord Jesus, I believe You are truly present in the Eucharist. I adore You, I love You, and I trust in You."

2. **Silence** – God's deepest words are spoken in silence; adoration trains the soul to listen.

   Spend several minutes in silence, letting one of Sheen's quotations echo in your heart. For example:

   "The greatest love story of all time is contained in a tiny white Host."

3. **Reparation** – Every Holy Hour consoles the Heart and Face of Christ for those who ignore or reject Him.

   Offer your Holy Hour for those who do not believe, do not adore, do not love Him.

Pray: *"O Lord, let the light of Your Face shine upon all souls, especially those who are far from You."*

4. **Transformation** – In adoration, we become like the One we behold; His Face is imprinted upon our souls.

   Close with Sheen's reminder:

   "The purpose of the Holy Hour is not to change God, but to change ourselves."

   Ask Christ to imprint His countenance upon your life, so that you may reflect Him to others.

5. **Mission** – The fire of evangelization is kindled before the Eucharist; adoration always sends us out renewed.

Prayers for Reflection

1. **Adoration:**

   "Lord, You are here, fully present in this Host. I gaze upon You, and I allow You to gaze upon me."

   O Jesus, truly present in the Most Holy Sacrament of the Altar, I adore You with all the love of my heart. Hidden under the veil of bread, You are the same Lord who walked among us, who suffered for us, and who rose in glory. I gaze upon You, and I let You gaze upon me. May this hour in Your presence bring light to my soul and peace to the world.

2. **Reparation:**

   "I console Your wounded Face, Lord, for every neglect and every indifference toward Your Eucharistic Presence."

   Lord Jesus, I come before Your Eucharistic Face to console You for the coldness, neglect, and ingratitude You suffer in this Sacrament of love. I unite myself to the sorrows of Your Sacred Heart and to the tears of Your Blessed Mother. Receive my prayers, my sacrifices, and my love as a small act of reparation, and through them, draw many souls back to Your merciful Heart.

3. **Transformation:**

"Let this time with You make me more like You. Shine upon me until Your Face is reflected in mine."

4. **Mission:**

"Send me forth as Your witness, Lord. May all who see me today see in me the reflection of Your Eucharistic Face."

5. **Prayer for Priests**

Eternal High Priest, Jesus Christ, I adore You in the Sacrament of the Altar and I intercede for all Your priests. Sanctify them, protect them, and fill them with the fire of Your love. May they be faithful to their daily Holy Hour, fervent in their ministry, and shining witnesses of Your Eucharistic Face to the world.

6. **Prayer for the Conversion of Sinners**

Merciful Jesus, by the light of Your Eucharistic Face, draw back to You all who wander in darkness. Heal wounded hearts, forgive sinners, and renew the world by the power of Your love. For their sake, I offer this hour in union with Your sacrifice on the Cross.

7. Prayer of Thanksgiving

Thank You, Lord, for this time with You. Thank You for the gift of the Eucharist, for the grace of Your mercy, and for the light of Your countenance. As I leave this holy place, may Your Face shine within me, so that others may see Your love reflected in my life. Amen.

Appendix III:
Prayers of Reparation to the Holy Face

Act of Reparation to the Holy Face

O adorable Face of my Jesus, so mercifully bowed down on Calvary for the love of us, I offer You the homage of my adoration, and I unite myself to the sorrow of Your Blessed Mother and all who love You. I beg pardon for all the outrages which are committed against You, especially those that wound Your holy countenance. Lord Jesus, imprint upon us the likeness of Your suffering Face, that we may bear in our souls the image of Your love and reparation. Amen.

Litany of the Holy Face

Response after each invocation:
"Have mercy on us."

- O Sacred Face of Jesus, sorrowful but radiant with love, **have mercy on us.**
- O Sacred Face, despised and dishonoured, **have mercy on us.**
- O Sacred Face, silently enduring blows and spittle, **have mercy on us.**

51

- O Sacred Face, crowned with thorns and bathed in blood, **have mercy on us.**
- O Sacred Face, shining with divine majesty on Mount Tabor, **have mercy on us.**
- O Sacred Face, radiant in the glory of the Resurrection, **have mercy on us.**
- O Sacred Face, the joy of angels and the delight of the saints, **have mercy on us.**

Closing Prayer:

Lord Jesus, we adore Your Holy Face. Shine upon us and grant us the grace to live and die in Your friendship. Amen.

Prayer of St. Thérèse of the Child Jesus and of the Holy Face

O Jesus, who in Your cruel Passion became "the reproach of men and the Man of Sorrows," I venerate Your divine Face on which shone the beauty and sweetness of the Divinity itself, until it was disfigured by the sins of men. Now I see it as if it were hidden beneath blood and tears. I desire to love You and to make You loved. May I draw souls to You and console Your Sacred Face by the innocence of my life, by my love, and by my sacrifices. Amen.

Offering of the Holy Face (St. John Vianney)

O Jesus, through the merits of Your Holy Face, have pity on us. Enlighten us, O Lord, by the splendour of Your countenance. Deliver us from all evil, and grant that we may ever fix our eyes upon You, so that we may be saved. Amen.

Short Ejaculatory Prayers of Reparation

(For silent repetition throughout the day)

- *"Lord, show us Thy Face, and we shall be saved."*

- *"O Lord, let the light of Your Face shine upon us."*

- *"Sacred Face of Jesus, have mercy on us."*

- *"O Jesus, may the memory of Your suffering Face be ever in my heart."*

- *"Eternal Father, through the Holy Face of Jesus, have mercy on us and on the whole world."*

54

Appendix IV:
Guide to a Holy Hour
of Eucharistic Reparation

Why Make a Holy Hour?

Archbishop Fulton J. Sheen often said: *"The Holy Hour is the hour that makes my day. Without it, I would not be able to preach Christ."* For sixty years, he spent one hour each day before the Blessed Sacrament, in silence, adoration, and reparation. He knew that the Church's greatest need was not more activity, but more intimacy with Christ in the Eucharist.

The Holy Hour is a time to be with Jesus, to gaze upon His Eucharistic Face, and to let Him gaze upon you. It is a time to console Him for the coldness, indifference, and ingratitude He suffers in the Sacrament of His love. It is also the time when He heals, strengthens, and transforms the soul.

How to Structure a Holy Hour

1. Preparation (5 minutes)

- Begin in silence. Make the Sign of the Cross slowly.
- Offer a short prayer of presence:
  "Lord, I am here. You are here. Let this time be Yours."

2. Adoration (15 minutes)

- Gaze upon the Host in silence. Allow the words of Scripture to stir your heart:
  "Be still, and know that I am God." (Psalm 46:10)
- Pray slowly: *"Lord, show me Your Face."*

3. Reparation (15 minutes)

- Offer prayers for sins against the Eucharist and against the Holy Face.
- Pray the Act of Reparation (from Appendix III).
- Unite your sorrows with the sorrows of Mary and Veronica, who consoled the suffering Face of Christ.

4. Intercession (10 minutes)

- Pray for family, friends, the Church, and the world.
- Offer special prayers for priests and for the conversion of sinners — Sheen's daily intention.

- Use Sheen's aspiration: *"Eternal Father, I offer You the Body, Blood, Soul, and Divinity of Your Son, truly present in the Eucharist, for the reparation of sins."*

5. Thanksgiving (10 minutes)

- Thank Jesus for His Presence, His mercy, and His love.
- Pray an Our Father, Hail Mary, and Glory Be slowly.
- Conclude with - *"Sacred Face of Jesus, may Your light shine upon me, upon the Church, and upon the whole world."*

6. Closing (5 minutes)

- Sit briefly in silence.
- Make the Sign of the Cross.
- Leave the chapel quietly, carrying His Presence into your day.

Tips for Making a Holy Hour

- **Be faithful, not perfect.** Don't worry about distractions; simply return your gaze to Him.
- **Use Scripture.** Read slowly from the Gospels or Psalms, especially passages on the Face of Christ.
- **Bring a prayer book.** Use the prayers in this volume when words fail.

- **Offer your hour.** Intend it for reparation, for priests, for sinners, for the needs of the world.
- **Be present.** More than anything, give Him your time and your heart.

Prayer to Begin a Holy Hour

Lord Jesus, I come before You in the Sacrament of Your love. I adore You, I thank You, and I desire to console You. Receive this hour as a small act of reparation for my sins and for the sins of the world. Shine upon me with the light of Your Face, and make me a faithful witness of Your love. Amen.

Appendix V:
Treasury of Hymns and Invocations

Traditional Eucharistic Hymns

O Salutaris Hostia

English:

1. O saving Victim, open wide
The gate of heav'n to us below.
Our foes press on from every side;
Your aid supply, your strength bestow.

2. To your great name be endless praise,
Immortal Godhead, One in Three;
Grant us, for endless length of days,
In our true native land to be.

Amen.

Latin:

1. O salutáris Hóstia,
Quae caeli pandis óstium:
Bella premunt hostília,
Da robur fer auxílium.

2. Uni trinóque Dómino
Sit sempitérna glória,
Qui vitam sine término
Nobis donet in pátria. Amen.

Tantum Ergo Sacramentum

English:

Down in adoration falling,
Lo! the sacred Host we hail;
Lo! o'er ancient forms departing,
newer rites of grace prevail;
faith for all defects supplying,
where the feeble senses fail.
To the everlasting Father,
and the Son who reigns on high,
with the Holy Ghost proceeding
forth from Each eternally,
be salvation, honor, blessing,
might and endless majesty. Amen.

Latin:

Tantum ergo Sacramentum
Veneremur cernui:
Et antiquum Documentum
Novo cedat ritui:
Præstet fides supplementum
Sensuum defectui.
Genitori, Genitoque
Laus et iubilatio,
Salus, honor, virtus quoque
Sit et benedictio:
Procedenti ab utroque
Compar sit laudatio.
Amen.

Adoro Te Devote

1. Godhead here in hiding whom I do adore
Masked by these bare shadows, shape and nothing more,
See, Lord at thy service low lies here a heart
Lost, all lost in wonder at the God thou art.

2. Seeing, touching, tasting are in thee deceived;
How says trusty hearing? that shall be believed;
What God's Son has told me, take for truth I do;
Truth himself speaks truly or there's nothing true.

3. On the cross thy godhead made no sign to men;
Here thy very manhood steals from human ken:
Both are my confession, both are my belief,
And I pray the prayer made by the dying thief.

4. I am not like Thomas, wounds I cannot see,
But I plainly call thee Lord and God as he:
This faith each day deeper be my holding of,
Daily make me harder hope and dearer love.

5. O thou, our reminder of the Crucified,
Living Bread, the life of us for whom he died,
Lend this life to me, then; feed and feast my mind,
There be thou the sweetness man was meant to find.

6. Like what tender tales tell of the Pelican,
Bathe me, Jesus Lord, in what thy bosom ran
Blood that but one drop of has the pow'r to win
All the world forgiveness of its world of sin.

7. Jesus whom I look at shrouded here below,
I beseech thee, send me what I thirst for so,
Some day to gaze on thee face to face in light
And be blest forever with thy glory's sight.

The Divine Praises

Blessed be God.
Blessed be His Holy Name.
Blessed be Jesus Christ, true God and true Man.
Blessed be the Name of Jesus.
Blessed be His Most Sacred Heart.
Blessed be His Most Precious Blood.
Blessed be Jesus in the Most Holy Sacrament of the Altar.
Blessed be the Holy Spirit, the Paraclete.
Blessed be the great Mother of God, Mary most Holy.
Blessed be her Holy and Immaculate Conception.
Blessed be her Glorious Assumption.
Blessed be the name of Mary, Virgin and Mother.
Blessed be St. Joseph, her most chaste spouse.
Blessed be God in His Angels and in His Saints.

Litany to the Sacred Heart of Jesus

Lord, have mercy Lord, have mercy.
Christ, have mercy Christ, have mercy.
Lord, have mercy Lord, have mercy.
Christ, hear us Christ, hear us.
Christ, graciously hear us. Christ, graciously hear us.

God the Father of Heaven, have mercy on us.
God the Son, Redeemer of the world, have mercy on us.
God, the Holy Spirit, have mercy on us.
Holy Trinity, One God, have mercy on us.

Heart of Jesus, Son of the Eternal Father, have mercy on us.
Heart of Jesus, formed by the Holy Spirit in the womb of the Virgin Mother, have mercy on us.
Heart of Jesus, substantially united to the Word of God, have mercy on us.
Heart of Jesus, of Infinite Majesty, have mercy on us.
Heart of Jesus, Holy Temple of God, have mercy on us.
Heart of Jesus, Tabernacle of the Most High, have mercy on us.
Heart of Jesus, House of God and Gate of Heaven, have mercy on us.
Heart of Jesus, burning furnace of charity, have mercy on us.

Heart of Jesus, vessel of justice and love, have mercy on us.

Heart of Jesus, full of goodness and love, have mercy on us.

Heart of Jesus, abyss of all virtues, have mercy on us.

Heart of Jesus, most worthy of all praise, have mercy on us.

Heart of Jesus, king and center of all hearts, have mercy on us.

Heart of Jesus, in whom are all treasures of wisdom and knowledge, have mercy on us.

Heart of Jesus, in whom dwells the fullness of divinity, have mercy on us.

Heart of Jesus, in whom the Father was well pleased, have mercy on us.

Heart of Jesus, of whose fullness we have all received, have mercy on us.

Heart of Jesus, desire of the everlasting hills, have mercy on us.

Heart of Jesus, patient and rich in mercy, have mercy on us.

Heart of Jesus, rich to all who invoke Thee, have mercy on us.

Heart of Jesus, fountain of life and holiness, have mercy on us.

Heart of Jesus, propitiation for our sins, have mercy on us.

Heart of Jesus, loaded down with opprobrium, have mercy on us.

Heart of Jesus, bruised for our offences, have mercy on us.

Heart of Jesus, obedient to death, have mercy on us.

Heart of Jesus, pierced with a lance, have mercy on us.

Heart of Jesus, source of all consolation, have mercy on us.

Heart of Jesus, our life and resurrection, have mercy on us.

Heart of Jesus, our peace and our reconciliation, have mercy on us.

Heart of Jesus, victim for our sins, have mercy on us.

Heart of Jesus, salvation of those who trust in Thee, have mercy on us.

Heart of Jesus, hope of those who die in Thee, have mercy on us.

Heart of Jesus, delight of all the Saints, have mercy on us.

Lamb of God, who taketh away the sins of the world, spare us, O Lord.

Lamb of God, who taketh away the sins of the world, graciously hear us, O Lord.

Lamb of God, who taketh away the sins of the world, have mercy on us, O Lord.

V. Jesus, meek and humble of heart.

R. Make our hearts like to Thine.

Let us pray:

Almighty and eternal God, look upon the Heart of Thy most beloved Son and upon the praises and satisfaction which He offers Thee in the name of sinners; and to those who implore Thy mercy, in Thy great goodness, grant forgiveness in the name of the same Jesus Christ, Thy Son, who lives and reigns with Thee, world without end. **Amen.**

Prayers and Invocations to the Holy Face

Invocation of Trust
Lord, show us Thy Face, and we shall be saved.

Invocation of Light
May the light of Your Eucharistic Face shine upon us, O Lord.

Invocation of Reparation
Sacred Face of Jesus, silently bearing insult and sorrow, have mercy on us.

Invocation of Mission
O Jesus, let the radiance of Your countenance be reflected in my life, that others may see Your love in me.

Invocation of Hope
Holy Face of Jesus, our light in darkness, our joy in sorrow, and our victory in trial, shine upon us now and forever.

Closing Aspiration

Lord, show us Thy Face.
And we shall be saved.

O Sacred and Holy Face of Jesus, radiant with love, shining in the Eucharist, bruised for our sins and glorified in the Resurrection — have mercy on us, and grant that one day we may see You face to Face in eternal joy. Amen.

Concluding Word:
Sent from the Light of His Countenance

To gaze upon the Face of Christ is not only to contemplate a mystery of faith but to encounter a living Presence. The Holy Face is not confined to an image or a memory; it shines forth most radiantly in the Eucharist, where Christ veils His glory under the humble appearances of bread and wine. Before the tabernacle or in the silence of adoration, the promise is fulfilled: we behold God face to Face.

Archbishop Fulton J. Sheen reminds us that every Holy Hour is a privileged moment when heaven bends low to earth, when the divine countenance gazes back at us with love. In the Eucharist, the bruised and glorified Face of Jesus looks upon us, inviting our hearts to be transformed.

As this book closes, let it open into worship. Kneel before the Eucharistic Lord, and pray with the Church: *"Lord, show us Thy Face, and we shall be saved."* May His Eucharistic radiance light our path in this life, and lead us one day to the unveiled vision of His glory for all eternity.

70

About the Author

Allan Smith is a Catholic evangelist, radio host, and spiritual director who has spent over a decade proclaiming the wisdom of Archbishop Fulton J. Sheen to audiences around the world. As the founder of Bishop Sheen Today, he has edited and published dozens of classic Sheen titles, including 'The Cries of Jesus from the Cross' and 'Lord, Teach Us to Pray'.

A passionate promoter of Eucharistic Reparation and devotion to the Holy Face of Jesus, Allan regularly speaks at parish missions, leads retreats, and hosts weekly radio broadcasts across Canada, the United States, Ireland, Australia and the Philippines. His work has helped reintroduce Sheen's powerful spiritual legacy to a new generation.

He lives in Canada with his family and continues his mission of calling souls to deeper intimacy with Christ through the example of saints like St. Thérèse of Lisieux and the timeless teachings of Fulton Sheen.

To learn more or to access free devotional resources, visit our two websites at:

www.bishopsheentoday.com

www.holyfacemiracle.com

About the Sheen Mission Series

The Sheen Mission Series is a four-volume spiritual journey inspired by Archbishop Fulton J. Sheen. Each book is designed as a devotional companion — guiding the faithful in prayer, reparation, and renewal through the Holy Face of Jesus, the Cross, the Eucharist, and the maternal love of Our Blessed Mother.

The series can be read in any order, yet together it forms a complete mission of grace:

- **Volume I – *The Holy Face and the Little Way***
  Walk with St. Thérèse of Lisieux in her Little Way of love, united to the devotion of the Holy Face of Jesus.

- **Volume II – *Behold Your Mother***
  Enter into Mary's tender care at the foot of the Cross and discover the strength of her Seven Sorrows.

- **Volume III –** *The Cross and the Last Words*
  Pray with Archbishop Sheen at Calvary as he
  opens the treasures of the Seven Last Words of
  Christ.

- **Volume IV –** *Lord, Show Us Thy Face and We
  Shall Be Saved*

  A mission of light and transformation, centred on
  the Eucharist and the saving power of Christ's
  Face.

*The Sheen Mission Series invites you to walk with
Archbishop Fulton J. Sheen in prayer, reparation, and
renewal – a journey of the Holy Face, the Cross, the
Eucharist, and Our Blessed Mother.*

J M J

A Personal Invitation

Over the years, I have had the privilege of helping souls draw closer to Christ through prayer, silence, and the beautiful wisdom of Archbishop Fulton J. Sheen.

If this devotional has nourished your heart, you may also find these works helpful in your journey of faith:

Advent and Christmas with Archbishop Fulton J. Sheen

- A Devotional Journey of Waiting, Welcoming, and Living the Mystery

Daily readings and gentle reflections to guide the heart from hope to joy — from the quiet longing of Advent to the radiant wonder of Christmas.

Priest, Prophet & King

- Meditations on Identity, Mission, and the Call to Holiness

Reflections on what it means to truly belong to Christ — in our families, vocations, and daily life.

The Sheen Mission Series
Collected Meditations

- Over 100 of the Richest Reflections from Retreats, Radio, and Prayer

A treasury to keep on the nightstand — for those ten-minute moments of quiet that become encounters with God.

May every book you read be an open door to the heart of Christ.

May these works draw you deeper into prayer, trust, peace, and surrender.

And may the Child of Bethlehem be born again in you.

Come, Lord Jesus.

To learn more or to stay connected:
www.bishopsheentoday.com

www.ingramcontent.com/pod-product-compliance
Lightning Source LLC
Chambersburg PA
CBHW061702120626
46550CB00003B/1054